W9-AQG-681

EUREKA!
I've discovered
ENERGY

Todd Plummer

 Marshall Cavendish
Benchmark
New York

Marshall Cavendish Benchmark
99 White Plains Road
Tarrytown, NY 10591
www.marshallcavendish.us

All Internet addresses were available and accurate when this book went to press.

Library of Congress Cataloging-in-Publication Data

Plummer, Todd.
I've discovered energy! / by Todd Plummer.
p. cm. -- (Eureka!)
Includes bibliographical references and index.
ISBN 978-0-7614-3202-9
1. Force and energy--Juvenile literature. 2. Power (Mechanics)--Juvenile
literature. I. Title.
QC73.4.P579 2008
531'.6--dc22
2008017058

Cover: Q2A Media Art Bank
Half Title : 1918 Internet Services/Istockphoto.
Thierry Maffeis/Dreamstime: P7; Andrzej Tokarski/Shutterstock: P11tl;
Bernard Maurin/Dreamstime: P11tr; Stillfx/ Shutterstock: P11bl; 1918 Internet Services/
Istockphoto: P11br; Diego Barucco/ Shutterstock: P15; J.Hester/ Arizona State University,
NASA/ESA: P19; William Fettes Douglas/The Bridgeman Art Library/Gettyimages;
The Print Collector/ Alamy: P24; Phdinbs/Istockphoto: P27; Fotoadamczyk/
Shutterstock: P27(inset top); Marty/ Bigstockphoto: P27(inset bottom).
Illustrations : Q2A Media Art Bank

Created by Q2AMedia
Creative Director: Simmi Sikka
Series Editor: Jessica Cohn
Art Director: Sudakshina Basu
Designer: Dibakar Acharjee
Illustrators: Amit Tayal, Aadil Ahmed, Rishi Bhardwaj,
Kusum Kala, Pooja Shukla and Sanyogita Lal
Photo research: Sejal Sehgal
Senior Project Manager: Ravneet Kaur
Project Manager: Shekhar Kapur

Printed in Malaysia

135642

Contents

Working It!

Energy is required to create **force**. A force makes things move or makes other kinds of changes. Whether a rocket is being launched or a snowflake is landing on the back of a lamb, energy is at work. At its most basic, energy is the ability to do work. When you mow the grass, that's work. Mowing grass takes energy. So you need to eat a good breakfast, which is another kind of energy.

The Nature of Energy

Energy can be converted from one form to another. For example, when you bake cookies in an electric oven, the oven converts electrical energy into **heat.** Heat is a kind of energy, too. The heat bakes the cookies. If you bake with a gas oven, there is a similar change in energy. Gas heat is produced when the oven burns a mix of gas and air.

Let's say you open the oven door to check and see if the cookies are done. Your friend checks, too, three minutes later. Some of the heat escapes into the kitchen each time the oven door opens. In one sense, the heat is lost. Yet the **Law of Conservation of Energy** says that no matter how energy gets changed and moved around, the total amount of energy in the universe never changes. The heat from the oven enters the kitchen instead.

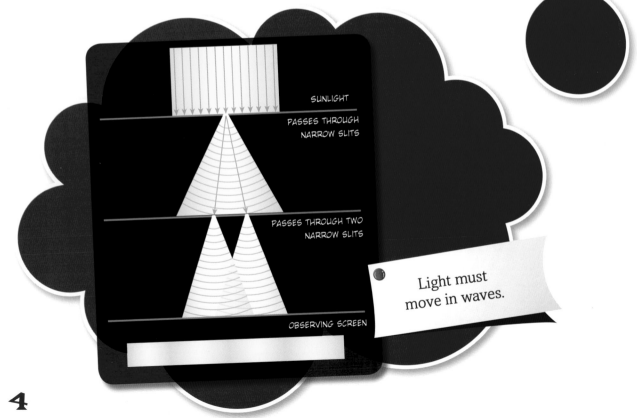

SUNLIGHT

PASSES THROUGH NARROW SLITS

PASSES THROUGH TWO NARROW SLITS

OBSERVING SCREEN

Light must move in waves.

Meet Dr. Thomas Young

Thomas Young (1773–1829) was an Englishman of many talents. He was a doctor, a musician, a language scholar, and an expert about Egypt. His studies about energy and especially light energy were famous. He was the first to use the word *energy* in the modern sense. Earlier scientists had decided that light was made from **particles**. Young's experiments showed that light was made of tiny waves. Eventually, other scientists proved that both ideas are right: Light is both a particle and a wave, depending on how you look at it.

CATCH MY MEANING?

SCIENCE

LANGUAGE

MATH

MUSIC

Greenhouse Effect

You Will Need:

2 clear jars of the same size

Lid to fit one of the jars

2 equal pieces of black construction paper, each about the width and height of the jars

Pen or pencil

Paper

2 thermometers (small enough to fit inside the jar with the lid closed)

1 Fold each piece of paper in half lengthwise. Put a piece of paper, which will absorb the sun, and a thermometer inside each jar. Arrange them the same way so you can read the thermometers without touching the jars.

2 Seal one jar with a lid, and leave the other one open. The jars will be placed in the Sun, and the closed jar will act like the atmosphere. The Sun warms Earth, and the atmosphere traps some of the solar energy.

3 Place the jars so sunlight hits the paper. Record the temperatures on the two thermometers every fifteen minutes for an hour. Don't open the sealed jar.

4 See how the sealed jar heats up faster due to heat energy trapped inside the jar. In the atmosphere, the amount of heat trapped depends on how many **greenhouse gases** are in the air. Those are gases such as carbon dioxide, which plants and cars produce.

WHO WOULD HAVE THOUGHT?

How hard would it be to make a **perpetual motion machine**? Such a machine would run forever with no added fuel or energy. It would have to produce more energy than it used. The Law of Conservation of Energy says it is impossible to build such a machine. Scientists have, however, developed a perpetual fountain. It is made from a strange substance: liquid helium cooled to almost **absolute zero**. Absolute zero is the total absence of energy. That happens at −460 degrees Fahrenheit, or −273 degrees Celsius. At that temperature, liquid helium acts very oddly. It climbs the walls of its container repeatedly. This perpetual fountain is fun to watch but is not much good as an energy source. Keeping the helium that cold uses too much energy.

Win Some, Lose Some

Cars and snow banks both have **mechanical energy**. That is the energy of motion. How can a snow bank have the energy of motion? Mechanical energy has two forms. A moving car has the energy of motion, or **kinetic energy**. A snow bank has stored energy, or **potential energy**. The snow bank could suddenly fall inward and rush down a mountain. If so, it would lose potential energy but gain kinetic energy. The car could stop, losing energy of motion, but gaining stored energy. It would lose kinetic energy but gain potential energy. The study of force and motion is called **mechanics**.

When two objects hit each other, energy shifts from one to the other. Think about a game of pool. A ball strikes another ball at rest. The moving ball stops. The other one takes off with the energy of the ball that hit it. **Gravity** plays a role in these energy transfers. Everything that happens has to work with or against gravity— even the sun as it dries drops of water.

Isaac Newton (1643–1727) was an English scientist who studied gravity and motion. He discovered laws of gravity and motion that govern the movements of everyday objects.

For people with patience, the world reveals how it works. Even **light**, observed closely, seems to **follow laws**.

Meet Galileo Galilei

Newton built his thinking on the work of Italian scientist Galileo Galilei (1564–1642). Galileo uncovered truths about the universe. He proved that the speed of a falling object depends on how long it's been falling, not how much it weighs. He showed that a moving object keeps moving unless another force slows it down. His observations of Jupiter's moons told him that the Sun, not Earth, was the center of the solar system. This discovery went against Roman Catholic Church teachings. The church said Earth was the center of everything. Italy was ruled by the church, so Galileo was put under house arrest.

Energy on the Move

You Will Need:

Bathroom scale

2 socks that can be ruined

3 pounds of rice

Measuring Cup

Yardstick

Friend

Rubber bands or twist ties to tie socks shut

1 Put a pound of rice in one sock and two pounds in the other sock. Tie the socks tightly shut with rubber bands or twist ties so no rice can get out.

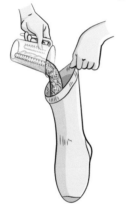

2 Falling objects change stored energy into energy of motion. To measure that, have your friend hold the yardstick next to the scale. Drop the one-pound sock from a height of one foot onto the scale. What's the highest weight that shows?

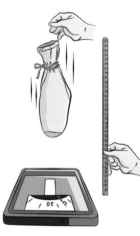

3 Drop the sock from 2 and 3 feet high, and check the weight each time. The more potential energy each sock and load has, the more kinetic energy the falling sock will have.

4 Measures of potential and **kinetic energy** also depend on the weight of the object. Use the two-pound sock and repeat the steps. Notice how the weight on the scale increases.

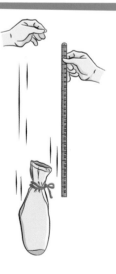

WHO WOULD HAVE THOUGHT?

Many common objects are considered **machines**. Staple removers, knives, door handles, hammers, and nails are all machines. Each has the same purpose: to make work easier. Most machines turn small forces into bigger ones by taking advantage of this rule:

Work = force × distance

For example, using a lever, you can apply 4 pounds of force over 5 feet (that's 20 foot-pounds) to lift a 20-pound weight one foot (also worth 20 foot-pounds). Other simple machines include ramps, gears, wedges (such as an axe), pulleys, and wheels.

Beat the Heat

The microwave beeps when your popcorn is ready. The cat naps in a splash of sunshine. The popcorn and cat are both made of **atoms** that are connected into units called **molecules**. The molecules dance around. The result of all that excitement is **thermal energy**. Thermal energy transfers between substances in contact with one another. The transfer is called heat. In the case of the popcorn, the microwave shoots beams of invisible light into the popcorn. The beams excite the water molecules inside. Steam builds inside the popcorn. That pops the kernels open. The cat gets heat from the Sun.

Thermal energy increases with temperature. **Temperature** is a measure of that heat. So temperature measures energy on the move. One of the many scientists and inventors who studied energy and temperature was William Thompson. He was also known as Lord Kelvin.

If he could tell his story . . .

Meet William Thompson (Lord Kelvin)

William Thompson (1824 –1907) was an Irish scientist. He did more than measure temperature in a new way. He used his knowledge in many practical ways. He helped design the first telegraph cable to go across the Atlantic Ocean. He made the first power station at Niagara Falls. He also spent years working to determine Earth's age. His final, best guess was that Earth was between twenty and forty million years old. In fact, Earth is more than a hundred times that old—or so we think now.

HE HAS A FEVER!

The year was 1848. I had a hot idea!

Daniel Fahrenheit had figured out that mercury would expand in heat. He had made a thermometer with mercury in it. He had made the freezing point of water 32 degrees on his thermometer.

Anders Celsius had figured out that a scale of 1 to 100 would be easier to use. He had made his own kind of thermometer, with zero the point at which water freezes.

Yet I knew we needed a more extreme scale, to measure extreme temperatures.

So I made zero the point that marks the absence of all thermal energy! I called that absolute zero.

Ice melts at 273 Kelvins, or K. Water boils at 373 K.

Heat Absorption

You Will Need:

String

2 balloons

Water

Candle

DO THIS ONLY WITH AN ADULT, and think about doing it outside. It can be smelly when balloons pop over a flame.

1 Get an adult's help to tie the balloons. Blow up one balloon and tie it closed. Fill the other balloon with water, and then tie it closed.

2 Have the adult light the candle and hold it up to the air-filled balloon. Count the seconds before the balloon pops. It won't take long.

3 Next, test the water balloon over a sink or go outside. Have the adult touch the flame to the balloon. Hold the candle to the balloon for a minute. The water will take in the heat. The heat will spread across the balloon's surface.

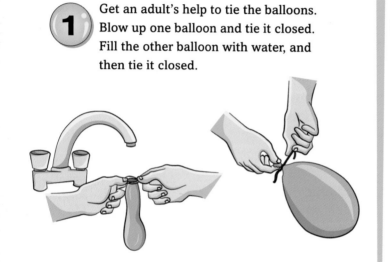

4 Consider: Water can take in a lot of thermal energy compared to other materials. As a result, bodies of water often affect the weather. If a body of water is warm, it acts on the cool air over the land nearby. If the water is cold, coastal areas will be colder than inland areas.

WHO WOULD HAVE THOUGHT?

You can tell the temperature and size of most stars by their colors. All stars are hot, but some are hotter—way hotter—than others. Bigger stars are hotter than smaller stars. Here is a scale for stars, from hottest to least hot. The temperatures are in Kelvins (K):

STAR COLOR	STAR CLASS	TEMPERATURE RANGE	SIZE* COMPARED TO THE SUN
Blue	O	30,000–60,000 K	18
Blue-White	B	10,000–30,000 K	3.8
White	A	7,500–10,000 K	1.7
Yellow–White	F	6,000–7,500 K	1.2
Yellow	G	5,000–6,000 K	1
Orange	K	3,500–5,000 K	0.75
Red	M	2,000–3,500 K	0.32

* The size is the diameter, or width, of a typical star of that class, divided by the diameter of the Sun. Our sun is a G-class star, in the middle of the chart. To see a blue-white star, view the constellation Orion at night. There is a blue-white star, named Rigel, in Orion's foot. There is a bright red star, named Betelgeuse, in Orion's shoulder.

Current Events

Electrical energy comes from the movement of **electrons**, which are tiny particles in atoms. These particles jump away from their atoms when the object they are part of can't hold any more of them. As they move from one object to another, they build up electricity. This electrical energy has two forms: electrical current or **static electricity**.

Electrical current is the flow of the moving electrons. We can direct this flow to places where we can use it. In our homes, electrical current powers many items, from refrigerators to ceiling lights. Static electricity is not a flow. It results when electron activity builds up on surfaces. Those annoying shocks you get after walking on carpet are from static. Lightning is static that builds between clouds or between clouds and Earth.

The scientist James Clerk Maxwell figured out that moving electrons cause not only electricity, but magnetism and light, too. Electrons in light move in waves at the speed of about 186,000 miles per second. Our eyes see light but cannot see its waves, because they go too fast. There are also light waves out there that our eyes cannot see. For example, X-rays and ultraviolet light from the Sun are invisible unless we use special machines.

Studying light and color go hand in hand. I ended up inventing the **color wheel** used by many artists.

Meet James Clerk Maxwell

James Clerk Maxwell (1831–1879) was a brilliant Scottish physicist. He made sense out of many earlier discoveries in electricity and magnetism. He had plenty of his own new ideas, too, which he gathered into one theory. In 1861, he used what he knew about color and light to make the first true color photograph. It was just a picture of colored ribbon, yet it was the start of something big. Einstein said that Maxwell's work was the most important in the field since Sir Isaac Newton. Maxwell also developed an important theory about the behavior of gases.

Don't Give Any Static

You Will Need:

Inflated balloon

Wool sweater

Water running
in a sink

Table salt

Ground pepper

Plate

1 Sprinkle a few shakes of salt and pepper onto a plate. Rub the balloon on the sweater.

2 Hold the balloon about a quarter of an inch over the salt and pepper. The salt appears to jump off the plate onto the balloon, but the pepper stays put. Electrical **charges** are positive, negative, or zero. Opposite charges attract each other. Similar charges push each other away. The electrons in the balloon have a negative (−) charge. That pushes the salt's negative electrons to the bottom of the salt bits.

3 The tops of the salt bits become positively (+) charged. They attract the balloon (−). The pepper's chemical structure works differently, so it stays put.

4 Now, rub the balloon and sweater again. Then, run the stream of cool water into the sink. Hold the balloon close to the stream. The stream of water actually bends toward the balloon for the same reason that the salt moved toward the balloon.

WHO WOULD HAVE THOUGHT?

A **gamma ray** burst has more energy than anything else in the universe. These bursts are created when huge stars cave in. For example, one star exploded recently in a distant galaxy. For a few months, it shot off more energy than 50 billion suns. That's more than all the energy of all the stars in some galaxies. Within our galaxy, the star called Eta Carinae has more energy than anything else. It is a big blue star that recently blew off a shell of gas (shown here). Some day this star could fall in, explode, and shoot gamma rays. Some scientists believe a similar event may have wiped out most animals 450 million years ago. That is before the dinosaurs walked Earth.

Molecules Rule

Your body changes food into energy. How? There is an attraction between positive and negative charges within a food molecule. That attraction makes a bond. These bonds have chemical energy. Break those bonds and that energy is released. When you eat the food, your body breaks the bonds. It converts the food molecules into energy your body can use.

Atomic energy works in a similar way. Every atom has a nucleus, or core. The core has one or more **protons**. Breaking a nucleus apart is difficult. You need a special collection of machines, known as a nuclear reactor, to do it. When a nucleus does break, a tiny amount of matter is changed into pure energy. That pure energy is awfully powerful, as can be seen in an atomic bomb.

Albert Einstein (1879–1955) was the scientist who made breaking an atom possible. He owed some of his thinking to John Dalton.

If Dalton could tell you . . .

Meet John Dalton

John Dalton (1766–1844) was English. Before Dalton, actual knowledge of elements and chemical processes had been a hopeless mess. There was a lot of misinformation. Old theories were based on incorrect ideas dating back to Aristotle. For centuries, **alchemists** had searched for something they called the philosopher's stone. They hoped to discover a way to turn basic metals into gold. So you can imagine the things they believed! They practiced a shady mix of science and magic. We now know that no such substance exists. Dalton's ideas about atoms and elements put an end to the old ways of thinking.

I worked for years, thinking about how the world worked.

I could see that each element had particular properties.

I started with the idea that atoms are indivisible. The Greek philosopher Democritus first put forth that idea long ago. He lived about 2,500 years ago.

Elements are basic substances of Earth, such as oxygen or iron. All atoms within an element are the same as the others. That is what makes an element an element!

Later, scientists figured out that what makes these atoms the same is the number of protons in the nucleus.

Chemistry at Home

You Will Need:

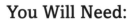

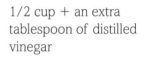

Meat, oven, candy, or science kit thermometer

Measuring cup

3 tablespoons of baking soda

1/2 cup + an extra tablespoon of distilled vinegar

1 Take one tablespoon of baking soda and place it in your measuring cup. Add a tablespoon of vinegar. Watch the reaction in the mix. The bubbles are carbon dioxide, the same gas that gives soft drinks their fizz.

2 Rinse out the cup and start over. Pour a half-cup of vinegar into the measuring cup. Put the thermometer in the vinegar. Check the temperature.

3 Measure two tablespoons of baking powder into the cup with the vinegar. Stir the mixture with the thermometer.

4 Watch the temperature quickly go up. Energy is released. The reaction sends chemical energy into the solution.

WHO WOULD HAVE THOUGHT?

The alchemists thought of gold and the sun as related. They thought of both gold and the Sun as the perfection of matter. While alchemists mixed substances, trying to create gold from other materials, they had little or no understanding of how atoms worked. We now know that the Sun and other stars run on nuclear energy. Stars are like huge nuclear furnaces. Their atoms go through bumps and crashes. The hits turn hydrogen atoms into helium atoms. How? In a string of crashes, four hydrogen nuclei join to make one helium nucleus. Every second, bits of matter from these reactions is converted into energy. That energy then shoots outward in all directions. Some of that makes its way to our planet, where it helps keep us warm and alive.

A Good Use of Energy

Y ou often hear that people need to conserve energy. That doesn't usually mean that people should sleep more. That doesn't have much to do with the Law of Energy Conservation, either. When people talk about conserving energy, they usually mean saving energy or using energy wisely.

Energy used to run machines, such as the electricity needed for a computer, has to be created from other sources. Those sources are often nonrenewable. That means they cannot be replaced. Nonrenewable sources include **fossil fuels**: oil, coal, and natural gas. Fossil fuels come from rotting plants and creatures buried in the ground. These fuels were created naturally but took millions of years to form.

Renewable energy sources include wind, the Sun, moving water, and burning wood. Wind, solar, and water energy have the extra benefit of being "clean energy." This means they don't produce the pollution and greenhouse gases that come from burning fossil fuels or wood.

If you heat your house with solar panels, you are not using gas or oil to warm your home. You are not adding to air pollution. The more you learn about energy sources, the easier it is to make decisions that can help our planet.

Imagine a world powered by sunlight.

Meet Augustin Mouchot

Augustin Mouchot (1825–1911) was a nineteenth century French mathematician. He was also a solar energy pioneer, proving once again that many "new ideas" are not so new. In 1860 Mouchot was concerned about his country's reliance on coal. You might say he got steamed about it! Mouchot invented the first solar generator that could convert solar energy into steam power. As time went on, he made his generator even better. By 1878, he could run a printing press with one of his solar-powered steam engines.

Catch the Wind

You Will Need:

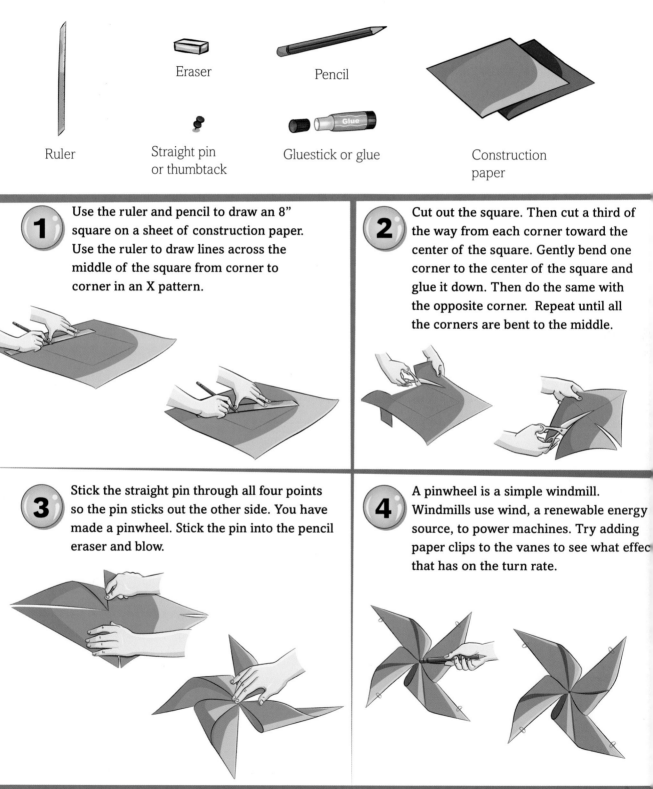

Ruler

Eraser

Pencil

Straight pin or thumbtack

Gluestick or glue

Construction paper

1 Use the ruler and pencil to draw an 8" square on a sheet of construction paper. Use the ruler to draw lines across the middle of the square from corner to corner in an X pattern.

2 Cut out the square. Then cut a third of the way from each corner toward the center of the square. Gently bend one corner to the center of the square and glue it down. Then do the same with the opposite corner. Repeat until all the corners are bent to the middle.

3 Stick the straight pin through all four points so the pin sticks out the other side. You have made a pinwheel. Stick the pin into the pencil eraser and blow.

4 A pinwheel is a simple windmill. Windmills use wind, a renewable energy source, to power machines. Try adding paper clips to the vanes to see what effec that has on the turn rate.

WHO WOULD HAVE THOUGHT?

Nearly all the energy on Earth starts out as solar energy. Fossil fuels such as oil, coal, and natural gas begin as plants. Plants convert sunlight into usable energy through **photosynthesis**. When plants die, the energy is stored in their cells. Over time, the plants rot and are covered by earth. The ground puts pressure on the rotting plants. That energy gets concentrated under pressure into those fossil fuels.

The Sun also dries water in oceans, lakes, and rivers. Clouds form and drop the water back to land as rain. That fills running rivers, which can be used for water power. Energy is flowing all around you, changing form and making life on Earth possible.

Timeline

1592
Galileo begins his experimental work on mechanics, geometry, and astronomy.

1686
Sir Isaac Newton publishes *The Principia*, which lays out the laws of motion and the theory of universal gravity.

1801
Thomas Young passes a beam of light through two slits, showing that light has the properties of a wave.

1805
John Dalton publishes his famous Atomic Theory of Matter. Alchemists lose their jobs almost overnight.

1905
Albert Einstein publishes his Special Theory of Relativity and explains that matter and energy can be converted into each other.

1864
James Clerk Maxwell presents his famous four equations of electricity and magnetism to the British Royal Society.

1848
William Thompson, Lord Kelvin, estimates the value of absolute zero based on the behavior of certain gases. He is off by less than half a degree.

1860
August Mouchot develops a solar-powered steam engine.

Glossary

absolute zero Total lack of molecular energy; equal to 0 K, −273°C, and −460°F.

alchemist Medieval philosopher who sought to discover methods to turn base metals like lead into gold.

atom Smallest possible particle of an element that has all the characteristics of that element.

charge In electricity, the positive, negative, or zero effect of a collection of electrons.

color wheel Arrangement of colors in a circle showing how the colors are related.

electricity Form of energy caused by the movement of electrons.

electron Particle of an atom that has a negative electric charge and orbits around the nucleus of the atom.

element Substance made of similar atoms that cannot easily be split into simpler parts.

energy Ability to create movement or some other kind of change.

force Anything that makes a push or a pull.

fossil fuel Substance such as oil, coal, and natural gas formed underground from plant material under high heat and/or pressure over millions of years.

gamma ray Most energetic form of light; invisible to human eyes.

gravity The pull that one (see entry for *mass*) exerts on another.

greenhouse gases Warming of Earth's lower atmosphere and surface due to solar heat trapped by the atmosphere.

heat Energy that flows from a warmer mass to a cooler mass.

kinetic energy Energy of any object that is moving.

Law of Conservation of Energy Law stating that energy may be changed from one form to another, but it cannot be created or destroyed.

machine Device that transmits force or changes motion, making it easier to do work.

mass The quantity of matter in an object, based on how many and what kinds of atoms it is made from.

mechanics Science that deals with energy and forces and their effects.

mechanical energy The amount of energy transferred by a force.

molecule Group of atoms held together by chemical bonds.

kinetic energy Energy of an object that is moving.

particle A very small piece or part.

perpetual motion machine Machine that can continue to move forever, or that puts out more energy than it takes in. It cannot exist according to the laws of physics.

photosynthesis Process by which plants use sunlight to make their own food from carbon dioxide and water.

potential energy Energy that is stored in an object and can be converted into other forms of energy.

proton Particle of an atom that has a positive charge.

renewable energy Energy that comes from sources, such as the wind or the sun, that do not run out or that can be refilled quickly.

static electricity Electrical charges that are built up on a material.

temperature Average thermal energy; degree of hotness or coldness of a substance.

thermal energy Energy that increases with temperature.

Index